Beyond Grief

Lessons in Love, Healing, and Growth

"A gentle companion in grief"

Mina Moore

Printed in the United States of America
First Printing, 2025
ISBN 979-8-9998678-0-3
Please send express written permission to:
Mina Moore | Sound Feels
 Panama City, Fl 32404
hello@minamoore.com

Dedication

Beyond Grief is dedicated to all that carry the invisible weight of loss and longing for peace. May you walk gently toward healing not to forget, but to remember who you are beyond the pain. May each intentional step and breath lead you closer to home, where your power, presence, and peace reside. You are not alone. You are deeply seen.

I wish you love and light throughout your journey.

> *Beyond grief, there is love reshaped, wisdom earned, and a path forward, one breath, one step, at a time.*

~Mina Moore

Preface

There was a time I moved through the world angry— carrying unspoken pain and unprocessed losses like invisible weights. I wore strength like a mask, smiling through survival, pretending I was fine when I wasn't. Just being her felt uncomfortable. But I didn't know another way.

The grief of losing my son cracked me open. His death was the hardest experience of my life. Through it, I met the quieter, heavier grief— the cumulative ache of losing not just him, but parts of myself along the way.

The girl I once was.
The woman I thought I had to be.
The dreams that never came to pass.
The love I didn't receive.
The love I didn't yet know how to give.

Loss doesn't always wear the face of death. Sometimes it's the absence of what could've been. The end of a relationship. The silence after trust is broken. The feeling of becoming a stranger to yourself. All of it lived inside me, buried beneath layers I didn't know were hiding my truth.

For a long time, I searched for the old me. I just wanted a glimpse, something familiar. But she was nowhere to be found. And eventually… I stopped looking.

Instead, I began peeling back the layers.

Choosing purpose.
Choosing presence.
Choosing to feel it all— the ache, the anger, the beauty, the healing.

This book is not a guide. It's not a formula. It's a reflection. A raw and honest collection of moments where I chose to keep going, even when I didn't know what healing would look like. It's born from sorrow and the slow remembering of who I am beneath it all.

A tribute to the version of me who kept surviving— and to the woman I'm becoming, unbound, authentic, and free.

Beyond Grief is not the end of pain, it's for the tender-hearted, the weary, the ones who've sat in the ruins and still reach for light. It's for those grieving someone they love, something they lost, or the person they used to be. It's a space where sorrow and hope can sit side by side, where healing is sacred, not linear. This is for anyone who has ever felt lost within themselves and dared to begin again, not as they were, but as they are becoming.

With gratitude,
With light,
With love...
~Mina Moore

Acknowledgements:

To my husband, Nolan, you have been the still point in the storm.

You have seen me at my most unrecognizable and still called me love.

When grief swallowed every being of who I thought I was, you stayed. Not to fix, but to witness. Not to hurry me, but to hold me.

Your love has been my anchor, your patience, a quiet kind of grace.

Thank you for seeing me when I couldn't see myself, for holding space for the unraveling and the rebuilding. I rose, again and again, because you never let me forget I could.

To my sons, you are my heart outside my body.

Your love has pulled me forward when my spirit wanted to stay still. Thank you for your grace. We're learning and healing together, growing into deeper love.

To my mother, your daily calls were lifelines–
small offerings of love and hope that reached me even in the silence.

You taught me resilience not just with your words, but with the way you live... steadfast, strong, and rooted in love.

Thank you for your support when I couldn't feel the ground beneath me.

To my siblings, thank you for holding space with love and laughter that reminded me I was not alone.

To my teachers, who offered wisdom, who offered challenge, who showed up exactly when I needed them...thank you for being the beacons that guided me back to myself.

And to every soul that has sat beside me in grief, in truth, in love this book is for you.

Your presence carried me through.

Table of Contents

Introduction:

Grief is a language no one teaches you how to speak. It arrives uninvited, reshaping everything you once knew with a force so profound that it leaves no part of you untouched.

When my son, Daquan, passed away, I was not just mourning him, I was mourning the version of myself that existed before that moment. Grief unraveled me, stripped me bare, and demanded that I rebuild from the inside out.

Grief is not just an ending. It is a teacher, a mirror, and, strangely, a form of love that refuses to disappear. In the early days, I fought against it, trying to outrun the pain, to fill the silence with distractions. But in time, I learned that healing does not come from avoidance, it comes from walking through the fire, from surrendering to the depths, and allowing grief to shape me into something new.

This book is not about "moving on." That phrase never sat right with me. How do you move on from love? Instead, this is a story about "moving through" grief, about learning to carry loss in a way that honors the love it stems from. It is about breaking cycles of pain, embracing mindfulness, and finding a way to exist in the world with both sorrow and joy.

Throughout this journey, I have uncovered lessons that have shaped me in ways I never expected. I have learned that grief is not linear, that healing is not about erasing pain but integrating it, and that we do not have to choose between holding on and letting go. In sharing my story, I hope to offer a light in the darkness, a gentle reminder that, even in the depths of loss, there is still room for love, growth, and transformation.

This book is for anyone navigating grief - for those who have loved deeply and lost profoundly. It is a companion for the moments when the weight feels unbearable, when the world seems too loud, or when you need a voice that understands.

I do not have all the answers, but I do know this: healing is possible. And together, we can walk this path beyond grief, not leaving love behind, but carrying it forward in a way that allows us to live and love fully once again. Six years ago, my world changed forever when my son, Daquan, left this earth. His love, light, and energy remain woven into everything I do.

This book – every guided meditation, every mindful moment, every step forward – is a tribute to him, a reminder that healing can transform the pain of grief into gratitude and purpose. That it is possible to make it through "The Other Side of Grief."

"The Other Side of Grief"

Grief came first – uninvited,
A storm that shattered every certainty.
Its weight pressed heavy,
A shadow clouding my world in gray.

Grief, though consuming,
Is a teacher wrapped in sorrow.
Its lessons, raw and relentless
Point to what truly matters:
Love, connection, the echoes that remain.

Through the haze of tears, specks of
light began to break through...

Not all at once, but slowly,
Like dawn sneaking up over a long, dark night.

Mindfulness became my anchor,
Breathing in resilience, exhaling pain.
I let go... not of love but of resistance.

As I embrace the ebb and flow of healing,
Grief's flames begin to fade, and
From its ashes, gratitude has appeared...

Gratitude for the love that loss has revealed,
For the memories etched deep in my soul,
For the strength born from this struggle.

Now, standing on the other side,
I see how grief gave birth to gratitude.

It's not an escape — but a transformation...
A sacred alchemy of heartache into hope,
Loss into love, sorrow into serenity.

Gratitude speaks now...

Not despite grief, but because of it.
It reminds me that life is unpredictable, chaotic at times, yet a beautiful
mess,

And even through the worst pain,
There is always something to be grateful for...

As I miss Daquan every day,
I choose to live... once more.

~Mina Moore

With Light, Love, and in Honor Of
Daquan Raphael Perkins
8/31/1993 - 2/1/2019

Chapter One

The Weight of Grief

Grief is heavier than anyone can prepare you for. It settles into your bones, turns every step into resistance — like wading through water.

It rewrites time too— some days stretch endlessly; others vanish in a blink.

In the early days after Daquan's passing, I felt like I was floating outside my own body— watching myself move through the world but not really living. Life continued. People smiled, traffic moved, the sun rose and set. But I was frozen, suspended between a past I couldn't return to and a future I no longer recognized.

No one tells you how grief rearranges everything. The air feels heavier. The light dims. Even the most familiar people and places start to feel like strangers.

Grief doesn't just change how you feel.

It changes who you are.

The Silent Language of Loss

There is an unspoken loneliness in grief. People mean well, but their words often miss the mark:

"He wouldn't want you to be sad."
"Everything happens for a reason."

They tried to comfort me with logic or hope, but what I needed wasn't words - it was presence. A silent space where my sorrow could simply exist, without needing to be fixed or explained.

Over time, I came to understand something profound: Grief isolates, but it also connects. There's a quiet recognition between those who've been there. It's in the way our eyes meet. In the pauses that say more than language ever could. Grief is deeply personal, but it carries a universal truth: Where there is great love, there will always be great loss.

How Grief Shows Up in the Body

What I did not expect was how grief would manifest physically: the exhaustion that sleep could not fix, the way my breath felt shallow, as if my body itself were resisting life. The tension in my shoulders, the aching in my chest, the emptiness in my heart. Science tells us that grief activates the nervous system, triggering fight-or-flight responses, but it felt deeper than that. **It was as if my body was mourning too.**

I started noticing that grief was not just emotional –it lived in my fascia, my heartbeat, my very breath. I was not just missing my son; my body was carrying the weight of that absence. And yet, even in that pain, my body was speaking to me, asking me to tend to it, to soften into the discomfort rather than resist it.

Surrendering to the Depths

At some point, I stopped fighting the grief. I let it wash over me. I allowed myself to cry without apology, to be present with myself, to sit in the silence without filling it, and to acknowledge the truth of what was lost without rushing toward a forced sense of "healing."

This chapter is not about solutions –it is about permission. Permission to feel, to fall apart, to honor the weight of grief without guilt. Before we can move beyond grief, we must first allow ourselves to fully experience it.

You are not broken for grieving deeply.
You are loving in a language the world doesn't always recognize.
Sometimes that love looks messy, fragmented, even unhinged.
But even in its sorrow, it is sacred.

> *When the weight feels unbearable, when the sorrow feels like too much to hold, return to your breath, where peace unfolds.*

Grounding Practice: Breathwork for Heavy Grief

1. Find a quiet space. Sit or lie down in a comfortable position. Close your eyes or soften your gaze and relax your shoulders.

2. Place your hands on your heart. Feel the rise and fall of your breath. Let yourself connect to the rhythm of your body.

3. Inhale deeply through your nose for 4 counts. Imagine drawing in light, warmth, or a sense of comfort.

4. Hold for 4 counts. Let this space be a pause –a moment of stillness within the storm.

5. Exhale slowly through your mouth for 8 counts. Release the weight, even if only for a moment.

6. Repeat for at least 5 cycles. Each breath reminds you: You are here. You are held. You are allowed to grieve and still be whole.

If tears come, let them. If silence is what you need, honor it. This practice isn't about fixing grief, it's about allowing yourself to exist within it, one breath at a time.

Reflections:

What emotions, memories, or sensations surfaced?

Take a moment to write down whatever arises after this breath practice.

Let your thoughts unfold onto the page. No judgement. Just flow.

_____

_____

_____

_____

_____

_____

_____

_____

_____

_____

_____

_____

_____

_____

_____

_____

It's Okay to Not Be Okay

There were days I couldn't get out of bed. Days I stared at the ceiling, paralyzed by the weight of my grief, and still, I survived. Healing isn't linear, and there is no map for the terrain of pain. There's only presence. There's only breath. There's only the moment in front of you.

I had to learn to stop judging my bad days. I had to make peace with my tears, my silence, my anger, my confusion. The truth is that grief doesn't always look like sadness. Sometimes it looks like numbness. Sometimes it looks like exhaustion. And all of it is valid.

Letting Go of the Pressure to Perform

We live in a world that glorifies resilience but often misunderstands what it really looks like. Strength isn't always loud. Sometimes, it's simply choosing to stay. To feel. To be honest. I gave myself permission to stop pretending. I didn't have to be strong for anyone. I just had to be real with myself.

The Sacred Pause

Not being okay opened the door to a deeper truth, I am worthy, even when I'm unraveling. I don't need to earn my rest or justify my pain. There is wisdom in stillness. There is strength in surrender.

So, if you're reading this and you're in that raw place, please know it's okay to not be okay. You don't have to fix it all today. You don't have to have answers. Just be here, exactly as you are. That's more than enough.

There will be moments when even breathing feels heavy, when your chest aches with memories and your mind spirals into doubt, fear, or numbness. In these moments, it's important to remember being "not okay" is not a weakness. It's a truth. And truths deserve to be honored, not hidden.

In the midst of every storm, just behind the darkest cloud, find solace in knowing the sun always shines again

Here are a few gentle ways I've learned to care for myself in those tender, overwhelming moments:

Pause and Acknowledge: Simply say to yourself, "This is hard." Naming the pain gives it shape and allows you to face it with compassion.

Ground Yourself: Place your hand on your heart or stomach. Feel your breath. Repeat: "I am here. I am safe. This will pass."

Reach Out: Not to fix or be fixed, but to be seen. A message to someone you trust, or a quiet moment in a support group, can ease the loneliness.

Do One Kind Thing: Drink water. Brush your teeth. Light a candle. Step outside. Tiny acts of kindness toward yourself are powerful acts of resistance against despair.

Give Yourself Permission: Rest. Cry. Retreat. Let go of the pressure to perform strength. You are allowed to fall apart and still be healing.

This is...Your Journey, Your Time, Your Way.

Some days you'll feel grounded. Others you'll feel lost again. But every step, forward and backward, still, is part of the journey.

Guided Meditation Practice:

A Gentle Return to the Heart for the moments you forget you are held.

Begin by sitting in a comfortable position. Let your body be soft. Let gravity hold you.

Soften your gaze. Place one hand on your heart, and the other on your belly. Feel the warmth of your own presence.

Take a slow, deep breath in… and exhale gently.

Let your breath be an anchor, steady and patient.

There is nowhere to be but here.

Now, whisper softly to yourself—silently or aloud:

"It's okay to not be okay."
"I give myself permission to feel."

Let those words float in your body like a gentle stream. Just be with what is.

Imagine a warm light surrounding you, soft, golden, and gentle. This light doesn't try to change your pain. It simply holds it, and you, with love.

Rest in this space. Stay for as long as you need.

When you're ready, bring your awareness back to the room. Wiggle your fingers, take a final deep breath.

Inhale... 5,4,3,2,1

Exhale...5,4,3,2,1

You've just given yourself a moment of peace.

Hold that with you.

Reflections:

What emotions, memories, or sensations surfaced?

Take a moment to write whatever arises after this meditation practice. Let your thoughts unfold onto the page.

No judgement. Just flow.

_____

_____

_____

_____

_____

_____

_____

_____

_____

_____

_____

_____

_____

_____

_____

Chapter Two

Grief is Love in Another Form

Grief is often described as an emptiness, a hollow space where love once lived. But over time, I've come to understand that **grief isn't the absence of love –it is love itself, transformed.** It's the love that has nowhere to go, the love that lingers in our cells, in our memories, in the spaces our loved ones once filled.

For a long time, I thought healing meant lessening my grief. I feared that if I stopped aching, it would mean I was forgetting. But grief is not something to be conquered. It is something to be carried, integrated, and honored. It exists because love existed first.

The Echo of Love

There are moments when I feel Daquan's presence in the smallest things, in the way the wind moves through the trees, in the song that plays at just the right time, in the sudden warmth that rushes through me when I speak his name aloud. It's as if love refuses to leave, finding new ways to remind me that it never truly disappears.

But the most profound reminders come through the birds. They arrive unexpectedly, perching nearby as if waiting for me to notice. Their songs, light yet powerful, weave through the air, carrying a presence that feels unmistakable. In their melodies, I hear Daquan – his laughter, his essence, the love that still surrounds me. Each time a bird visits, I am reminded that love does not simply vanish. It shifts, it sings, and it finds its way back to us in ways we least expect.

Love is energy, and energy cannot be destroyed. Science tells us this, but so does the heart. The love I have for him didn't vanish the day he left this world. It expanded, deepened, and took on a new form. And sometimes, love has wings.

Guilt and the Fear of Moving Forward

One of the hardest lessons grief has taught me is that moving forward does not mean moving away. At first, any moment of joy felt like betrayal. I questioned whether I had the right to smile, to dream, to find peace when my son no longer walked this earth. I had to learn that grief **and joy can coexist**. One does not erase the other.

Guilt whispers that to heal is to forget, but that is a lie. Healing is simply learning how to live with love in a new way. It is allowing love to evolve, to stretch beyond the boundaries of physical presence, and to explore the depth of more.

Keeping Love Alive in a New Way

Grief invites us to create new rituals and find new ways of keeping love alive. Maybe it's lighting a candle, speaking their name, writing letters, or simply pausing in the quiet to feel their presence. For me, it has been through sound – through the vibrations that connect us beyond what is seen.

To anyone carrying grief: your love has not been lost, only changed. It is still here, woven into your breath, your heartbeat, your existence. The weight of it may feel unbearable at times, but that weight is proof of something sacred.

> **The culmination of love is grief, and yet we love despite the inevitable. We open our hearts to it... To grieve deeply is to have loved fully. Open your heart to the world as you have opened it to me, and you will find every reason to keep living in it.**

- Fay, God of War Ragnarök

Reflection Practice: Honoring the Love Within Grief

When grief feels overwhelming, take a moment to transform it back into love. Begin to open your heart to the world again with this practice:

1. Sit in stillness. Close your eyes, place a hand over your heart, and take a slow, deep breath.

2. Think of a moment of love. A memory that makes you smile, a time when you felt connected to your loved one.

3. Speak their name aloud. Let it vibrate in the air, carrying love with it.

4. Whisper a message anything you wish they could hear. Trust that they do.

5. Breathe in gratitude. Acknowledge the love that still exists, even in their absence.

> *Grief is love in another form. Let it remind you always, that love endures.*

Reflections:

What emotions, memories, or sensations surfaced?

Take a moment to write whatever arises after this breath practice. Let your thoughts unfold onto the page.

No judgement. Just flow.

_____

_____

_____

_____

_____

_____

_____

_____

_____

_____

_____

_____

_____

_____

Chapter Three

Healing is Nonlinear

ealing doesn't follow a straight path. There is no roadmap, no clear beginning or end. Grief comes in waves – some gentle, others crashing with storm-like force. One day, you feel steady, as if you've learned how to carry the weight. The next, a scent, a song, or an unexpected memory pulls you under again.

For a long time, I thought I was doing grief "wrong." I believed healing meant a steady climb upward, a gradual lessening of the pain. But grief doesn't work that way. It loops back, circles around, and revisits places you thought you had already left behind. Healing is not about moving in a straight line – it's about learning how to navigate the highs and lows, the spirals, and everything in between.

Today, I had to fight…
Fight to get up.
Fight for my sanity.
Fight for light.
Fight for love.
Fight for hope.
Fight for healing.
Fight for joy.
And even when my strength felt thin, I remembered…
Every breath is a victory.
Every tear that falls is a release.
Every step, no matter how small, is still a movement toward healing.
So, keep fighting…because peace is worth it, joy is worth it, I am worth it, and you are worth it. Keep moving forward, never give up

The Illusion of 'Moving On'

People often talk about "moving on" as if grief is something to leave behind. But how do you move on from love? The truth is, we don't move on — we move forward, we move through, carrying our love, our memories, and, yes, our grief, in new ways.

There were days when I felt like I had made peace with Daquan's passing, only to wake up the next morning in a flood of sorrow. At first, I saw this as a failure. But I now understand that each return to grief is not a setback — it's a deepening, a breakthrough. Each time grief rises again, it offers another layer of healing, another chance to integrate the love that remains.

Grief Comes in Seasons

Just as nature shifts through seasons, so does grief. There are winters of deep sadness, where the world feels frozen in loss. Springs of renewal, where moments of joy peek through. Summers where love feels vibrant again.

And autumns where memories drift in like falling leaves, reminding us of both beauty and impermanence.

Some seasons last longer than others. Some return when we least expect them. But none of them are final. **Grief is not a single moment in time; it is a lifelong unfolding — a forever journey.**

Trusting Your Own Timeline

Healing is deeply personal. Some find solace in prayer and meditation, others in movement, in nature, in creative expression. There is no single way through. The only truth is that healing is yours to define, at your own pace.

If today is a day when grief feels too heavy, let it be. If tomorrow brings a glimpse of light, welcome it without guilt. If you find yourself returning to sorrow after a period of peace, know that this is not starting over, it is simply another step in the journey.

Reflection Practice: Embracing the Spiral of Healing

When grief feels like it's circling back, instead of resisting, try this gentle reflection:

1. **Find a quiet space.** Sit with your grief like an old friend—with no judgment, no rush.

2. **Place a hand over your heart.** Feel your heartbeat, steady and alive. Remind yourself: "I am still here. There is no rush. I am still healing."

3. **Ask yourself:** What is grief showing me today? Embrace what shows up, even if it doesn't make sense yet.

4. **End with a breath.** Inhale deeply, hold for 4 counts, exhale slowly for 8 counts. Sit with it for as long as you need. Trust that healing is happening, even in the moments that feel like it's not.

You are not moving backward. You are unfolding, step by step, into deeper understanding, into love that never leaves.

> **Affirm: This is my journey. I create space for healing and transformation at my own pace, in my own time.**

Reflections:

What emotions, memories, or sensations surfaced?

Take a moment to write whatever arises after this breath practice. Let your thoughts unfold onto the page.

No judgement. Just flow.

_____

_____

_____

_____

_____

_____

_____

_____

_____

_____

_____

_____

_____

_____

_____

Love your darkness and you shall know your light

-Vironika Tugaleva

Chapter Four

Pain Was a Teacher

P ain is something I was taught to avoid. From an early age, I was conditioned to push it away, to be strong, to numb it, and to seek distractions just to avoid feeling it. But grief has no shortcuts.

It demands to be felt. And in that deep, aching sorrow, I learned something unexpected: **pain, when honored, becomes a teacher.**

Losing Daquan shattered me, but within the pieces, I began to see truths I had never fully understood. Pain stripped away the noise, revealing what mattered most. It made me confront myself, my patterns, my fears, and my ability to love – even through loss.

Pain is Not the Enemy

For a long time, I resisted my grief. I fought against the waves, trying to stay afloat through sheer force of will. But pain is like the ocean – the more you fight it, the more it pulls you under. The moment I stopped resisting; I found I could float.

Pain is not here to punish us. It is here to show us something: about ourselves, about love, about the depths of our resilience. When I stopped running from my grief, I began to understand it. I stopped asking, "Why did this happen to me?" and started asking, "What can this teach me?"

The Lessons Within Suffering

Pain has a way of revealing truth. Here are some of the lessons it taught me:

- **Presence is everything.** When the future feels unbearable and the past is too painful, the present moment is the safest place to be

- **Love does not disappear.** Grief is proof of love's endurance – even beyond this life.

- **I am stronger than I thought.** There were days I didn't think I could survive the weight of loss. And yet, I did.

- **Suffering deepens compassion.** Grief cracked me open, but in that openness, I learned how to hold space for myself and others in ways I never could before.

- **Healing requires surrender.** Not to the pain itself, but to the process —allowing it to move through me rather than burying it.

Finding Meaning Without Justifying Loss

One of the hardest parts of grief is the search for meaning. The world tells us, "Everything happens for a reason", but that never sat right with me. Some losses are simply cruel. Some pain cannot be explained.

Here's what I've learned in not understanding "why": We can still find meaning. I don't believe Daquan was meant to leave this earth so soon. I do believe that his love, his spirit, and the lessons he left behind continues to shape me. His presence guides the way I live, the way I heal, the way I choose to keep moving forward – not because I must, but because his love pushes me to.

Pain is not meant to be carried forever. It is meant to shape us, to teach us, and eventually, to soften into something else: understanding, compassion, even wisdom.

> *Listen, feel, let the lessons guide you*

Healing Practice: Sitting With Pain, Not in It

Try this practice to allow pain to move through you instead of staying stuck within you.

1. Find a comfortable place to sit. Close your eyes and take a deep breath in, then exhale slowly.

2. Acknowledge the pain. Instead of pushing it away, simply name it: I see you. I feel you. I allow you to be here.

3. Visualize your pain. Is it heavy? Does it have a shape, a color? Without judgment, observe it.

4. Now imagine it softening. Like waves returning to the shore, let the pain expand and release, little by little. Visualize yourself floating to the shore.

5. Place your hand over your heart. Whisper to yourself: I am not my pain. I am the love that remains.

Reflections:

What emotions, memories, or sensations surfaced?

Take a moment to write whatever arises after this breath practice. Let your thoughts unfold onto the page.

No judgement. Just flow.

_____

_____

_____

_____

_____

_____

_____

_____

_____

_____

_____

_____

_____

_____

_____

_____

Chapter Five

You Are Not Alone

G rief has a way of making the world feel smaller. It isolates, not just because others may not understand, but because in deep sorrow, even the most familiar spaces feel foreign.

I remember walking into rooms and feeling invisible, as if the weight I carried was something only, I could see.

Grief, though deeply personal, is also universal. And if there's one thing I've learned, it's this: *we are never truly alone in our sorrow.*

Loneliness of Loss

After Daquan passed, there were days when I felt like I was the only person in the world experiencing this depth of pain. The world outside continued – people laughed, worked, lived their lives – but my world had stopped.

Well-meaning friends and family offered words of comfort, but sometimes their words felt distant, as if they couldn't reach the place I had fallen into. And then there were those who disappeared – those who didn't know what to say and said nothing at all.

Loneliness in grief isn't only about being alone physically; it's about feeling unseen, misunderstood, like the weight of your loss exists in a world that no longer knows how to hold it.

The Quiet Presence of Others

In the depths of my solitude, I started noticing something else: the small moments where connection still found me.

The stranger who offered a kind smile when I felt unseen.
The friend who sat with me in silence, expecting nothing.
The birds who visited me with their songs, reminding me that love never truly leaves.

Grief connects us in ways we don't always realize. There are others who have felt this ache, who understand without words. And while no one can take the weight of loss from us, we don't have to carry it alone.

Seeking and Allowing Support

For a long time, I believed I had to grieve in silence, that my pain was mine alone to bear. Healing, I've learned, happens in community. **It's okay to ask for support and it's okay to accept it.**

Whether through loved ones, grief circles, therapy, or even unexpected moments of connection with strangers, there are hands willing to hold yours, voices willing to listen, and hearts that understand.

Building a New Community

One of the hardest truths about grief is that it changes relationships. Some friendships fade – not out of malice – but because loss reshapes us, and not everyone knows how to meet us where we are. However, grief also opens the door to new connections, ones rooted in a deeper understanding, a shared knowing.

Finding your people after loss may take time, but they are there. The ones who won't rush your healing, who will sit in stillness with you, who understand that grief doesn't need to be fixed, only honored. The ones who respect your boundaries, giving you space when needed but never abandoning you because of it. Support comes from those who understand that setting boundaries isn't rejection, it's self-preservation. They stay, they hold space, they meet you where you are without conditions, judgement, or timelines. ***You are not alone in this. Even in the quietest moments, love surrounds you.***

> **There is no "normal" way to grieve. Except for how we each do it.**
>
> **- Melvina Young**

Healing Practice: A Letter to Your Grief Community

When grief feels isolating, take a moment to acknowledge those who have supported you – whether seen or unseen.

1. Write a letter. Address it to anyone who has held space for you in your grief: a friend, a loved one, even nature, animals, or the universe itself.

2. Express gratitude. It doesn't have to be grand, simply acknowledging their presence is enough.

3. Include yourself. Thank yourself for surviving, for showing up, for carrying love through loss.

If no one comes to mind, that's okay. Instead, write to the future – to the people you will meet, the connections that will come, the love that will find its way back to you. Because even in grief, love always finds a way

Reflections:

What emotions, memories, or sensations surfaced?

Let your thoughts unfold onto the page.

No judgement. Just flow.

_____

_____

_____

_____

_____

_____

_____

_____

_____

_____

_____

_____

_____

_____

_____

_____

Chapter Six

Mindfulness & Presence in Grief

G rief has a way of pulling us away from the present. It tethers us to the past, where memories replay like an endless loop, or drags us into the unknown of the future, filling us with fear, regret, and uncertainty. In the early days of my grief, I found myself caught in both—longing for what once was while dreading what was to come. The weight of it all felt unbearable, so I created a version of myself just to survive, one that buried the pain beneath unhealthy behaviors, distraction, and avoidance.

But that version wasn't truly serving me. It was a shield—one that kept me disconnected not only from my pain, but also from my healing.

Mindfulness became the bridge that led me back to myself. It helped me cultivate self-awareness and taught me to be present, even when it hurt. Slowly, I began to see that I didn't have to run anymore. I didn't have to numb or avoid. I could begin again—one breath, one sound, one moment at a time.

At first, presence felt unbearable—too quiet, too full of reminders, too quiet, too full of reminders, too empty of his voice. But over time, I learned that presence wasn't about pushing the pain away. It was about learning to be with it—to soften toward it, to breathe through it, and to listen. Not just with my ears, but with my whole body.

The Sound That Saved Me

There was a time when silence felt like punishment. The stillness in the house was so loud it echoed. But when I first picked up a singing bowl and let the vibration ring through the room, something in me stirred. It wasn't about music. It was about frequency. About resonance. About the feeling that even though everything had changed, something ancient and steady was still vibrating beneath it all.

Sound became my medicine—tones and vibrations that bypassed my busy, grieving mind and spoke directly to my nervous system, to my heart, to my spirit. Tuning forks, crystal bowls, ocean drums... each one opened a new doorway back to me.

The science behind sound healing is simple yet powerful: your body is a symphony of vibration. Every cell, every breath, every heartbeat carries a rhythm. When we introduce certain frequencies—like the ones produced by singing bowls or the human voice—we help regulate the nervous system, slow brainwave activity, and invite the body into a parasympathetic (rest and digest) state. That's where healing begins.

But for me, it was more than science. Sound helped me grieve. It helped me remember. It became a sacred space where I could cry, scream, pray, or just be. No fixing. No rushing. Just sound and surrender.

Breathing Through the Pain

One of the first things grief takes from us is our breath. In the depths of sorrow, I noticed how shallow and constricted mine had become, as if my body was bracing for impact—preparing for a storm that had already arrived. The weight in my chest was so heavy at times that I didn't want to breathe at all.

But it was the breath that reminded me I was still here. Still living. Still capable of feeling something other than despair.

I began practicing conscious breathwork in small ways—just noticing my inhale and exhale. Over time, I learned techniques that supported emotional release and nervous system regulation. Some breaths brought me into stillness; others cracked me open and allowed old grief to pour out.

The breath is the body's first language. When we pay attention to it, we begin to understand what's happening underneath the surface. It tells us when we're scared, when we're shutting down, when we're safe. And it always brings us back to the present.

Every time I returned to my breath, I reclaimed a piece of myself. Each breath became a prayer: I'm still here. I choose to stay. I choose to heal.

The Power of Simply Being

When I first began practicing mindfulness, it wasn't about trying to "fix" my grief. It was about learning to sit with it, to see my pain without trying to push it away. Some days, that looked like sitting in silence, listening to the wind through the trees. Other days, it meant letting the birds' songs

47

remind me that I was still here, still connected, still breathing.

Mindfulness isn't about avoiding grief—it's about making space for it without being consumed by it. It's the gentle noticing of what is. It's the permission to feel without judgment, to let tears fall, to hold your sorrow with tenderness instead of resistance.

Presence didn't erase the pain, but it gave me the strength to carry it differently—with acceptance, compassion, and a deeper understanding of myself.

Meditation as Sacred Reconnection

I used to think meditation was about escaping. Clearing the mind. Floating somewhere far away. But grief taught me that meditation is about coming home. It's about sitting with what is, without needing to change it. It's about making space for the sorrow, and for the love that still exists underneath it all.

At first, sitting in silence felt impossible. My thoughts raced. My heart ached. But over time, I realized that meditation didn't need to look like perfect stillness. Sometimes, I meditated through tears. Sometimes through chanting. Sometimes with my hands on my heart, just breathing.

And in those quiet moments, I began to feel my son again—not just in memory, but in energy. In presence. In love. Meditation became a doorway to the sacred. To connection. To remembering.

Pain into Purpose

These practices—sound, breath, and meditation—didn't erase my grief. They transformed my relationship to it. They helped me carry it, hold it with compassion, and walk with it as a part of me, rather than something I needed to fight or fix.

Eventually, what supported my healing became part of my purpose. I began sharing these tools with others—offering sound journeys, guided breathwork, and meditations for those navigating their own losses. Not from a place of having it all figured out, but from a place of walking this path with them.

Mindfulness in grief isn't about perfection or peace that never wavers. It's about being willing to return to the present moment, again and again— even when it's hard. It's about finding anchors—like breath, sound, and stillness—that can hold us while the waves of sorrow rise and fall.

And it's about remembering, always, that healing doesn't mean forgetting. It means learning to live with love and loss in the same breath.

A Breathwork Practice for Heavy Moments

1. Close your eyes. Place one hand on your heart, the other on your belly.

2. Inhale deeply through your nose for 4 counts. Feel your belly expand.

3. Hold for 4 counts. Let the air settle within you.

4. Exhale slowly through your mouth for 6 counts. Release the weight – even if only for a moment.

5. Repeat for five cycles. Each breath is a reminder: I am still here. I am still healing.

> **Sometimes it's okay if the only thing you did today was breathe.**

–*Yumi Sakugawa*

Finding Presence in Everyday Moments

Grief can make the world feel distant, like you're walking through a dream that doesn't quite belong to you. Everything looks the same, but nothing feels familiar. In these moments, mindfulness becomes a lifeline — not a cure or a fix, but a quiet hand on your shoulder — reminding you that you are still here. That life, though changed, continues. Presence doesn't erase pain, but it makes room for it. And in that space, healing begins.

Here are some quiet ways to return to the present, even in the thick of loss:

Touch Something Grounding

Place your hand on the bark of a tree. Feel its age, its stillness, its rootedness. Pick up a rock and notice its weight, its coolness, its quiet strength. Run your fingers over the weave of a favorite piece of fabric. Let the texture remind you that you are still part of the physical world — that your body belongs here, even in sorrow. These small gestures reconnect you with what is real and solid. They whisper: You are here. You are held. You are healing.

Engage Your Senses

Open yourself to what's around you. Let the warmth of sunlight on your skin remind you of softness. Inhale the scent of rain on the pavement or freshly turned soil. Taste something simple and comforting. Notice how the air feels — crisp, humid, heavy, or light. The world is still alive, still turning, still offering its beauty in quiet ways. Allow your senses to draw you gently back into the now.

Listen

Let your ears tune in to life's subtler sounds: the hush of wind through trees, birdsong in the early morning, the rustle of your own breath. Listen to music that speaks the language of your heart and let it move through you like water. Sit in silence and notice the space between sounds. There's a kind of presence in stillness that asks nothing of you. Just be. Let yourself be held in that sacred quiet. Let the act of listening bring you back to yourself.

Speak Their Name

Say it softly. Say it out loud. Say it often, even if your voice trembles. Let the sound of it fill the air again. Let their memory live not just in your thoughts but in your breath. Speak to them if you need to. Whisper your love, your sorrow, your gratitude. In speaking their name, you honor their presence. You create space for them in the here and now – not only in the past.

Take Mindful Walks

Move slowly. Let your feet carry you with intention, not toward a destination, but into awareness. Step by step, let the rhythm of walking become a meditation. Breathe in where you are. Notice the colors around you, the shape of the sky, the rhythm of your stride. Let walking become a quiet ritual of remembrance – a way to carry grief gently, without being consumed. Each step is a prayer, a reminder, you are still moving, you are still here. In walking with presence, you carry your grief not as a burden, but as a companion on the path to healing.

Embracing Grief with Awareness

Mindfulness doesn't take grief away, but it allows us to hold it differently. It reminds us that while the past shaped us and the future is uncertain, **the present is the only place where healing happens.**

If all you can do today is take one breath, notice one thing, or be present for one small moment—that is enough. That is healing.

Healing Practice: A Moment of Stillness

When grief feels overwhelming, try this short practice:

1. **Find a quiet space.** Sit comfortably, with feet planted or lying down.

2. **Close your eyes and take a deep breath.** Feel the air enter your lungs.

3. **Place your hands over your heart.** Feel its rhythm, steady and strong.

4. **Whisper a word or phrase.** I am here. I am safe. I am allowed to grieve.

5. **Stay in stillness for a moment.** Let yourself be exactly as you are — without judgment.

Grief asks us to be present with our pain. And in that presence, we find love, memory, and the quiet strength to keep going.

Reflections:

What emotions, memories, or sensations surfaced?

Take a moment to write whatever arises after this breath practice. Let your thoughts unfold onto the page.

No judgement. Just flow.

Chapter Seven

Creating New Narratives

G rief changes the way we see ourselves. It rewrites the story we once talked about our lives, about our future, about who we thought we were. After Daquan passed, I felt like I was living in a version of my life I never agreed to, a story that had been ripped from my hands and rewritten by loss.

For a long time, I felt trapped in that version, my identity had felt tethered to my grief, as if I was nothing more than the mother of a son who was no longer here. Grief is not meant to define us; it is meant to transform us. We do not erase the love, but we do get to decide how we carry it.

At some point, I realized, I could hold on to my pain, or I could create a new narrative – one that honored my grief but did not let it consume me.

> ## *It's not about waiting for the storm to pass, it's about learning to dance in the rain.*

— Anonymous

This quote spoke to me as I gained insight into embracing the messy parts of healing, helping me to realize that I could hold on to my pain, or *I could create a new narrative — one that honored my grief, and more importantly honored the memory of my son.*

The Stories We Tell Ourselves

Our minds are constantly narrating our lives. In grief, those stories can become heavy:

- I will never feel joy again.
- I am broken beyond repair.
- My life ended the day they left.

These thoughts feel real, but they are not the only truths available to us. Grief is part of our story, but it is not the whole story.

I began to ask myself: What if I could rewrite this? What if I could create a narrative that allows both grief and growth to coexist?

"I laughed I cried
I've lived I've died
Reborn...
I realize
I am the keeper of my joy"

Rewriting the Narrative

Healing doesn't mean letting go; it means making space for something new. Here's how I began to shift my story:

1. Acknowledging the pain but not letting it define me.

- Instead of "I will never heal," I began to tell myself, "I am learning to live with love and loss."

2. Finding purpose within my pain.

- I asked: What can I create from this? This book, my healing work, and the way I connect with others – all of it is part of my new story.

3. Speaking of my son in a way that honors his life, not just his absence.

- Instead of only focusing on the loss, I chose to focus on the love. I celebrate who he was, what he taught me, what he continues to teach me, and how he still lives within me.

4. Allowing joy to return without guilt.

- Grief told me happiness was betrayal. But I am learning joy is not the opposite of grief, it is proof that love continues.

Who Are You Becoming?

Loss changes us, but we get to decide how. Grief asks us to reflect:

- Who am I now?
- How has this experience reshaped me?

- What do I want my story to be moving forward?

It's okay if you don't have answers yet. Just know this: You are still here, and your story is still unfolding.

Reflection Practice: Writing a New Narrative

Write a letter to yourself.

1. Begin with where you are now. Acknowledge your grief, your pain, your truth.

2. Imagine the person you are becoming. What do they feel? What do they believe?

3. Write as if you are already stepping into this new version of yourself. Instead of *"One day, I hope to heal,"* try *"I am learning how to carry love and loss with grace."*

> *"Your grief is real. But so is your strength. You are allowed to write a story that includes healing"*

Let your thoughts unfold onto the page.

No judgement. Just flow.

_____

_____

_____

_____

_____

_____

_____

_____

_____

Chapter Eight

The Power of Ritual & Memory

Grief has a way of making time feel disjointed. The past feels too far away, yet the loss feels like it just happened. Some memories bring warmth, others an ache so deep it's hard to breathe. And yet, memory is one of the greatest gifts we have — it allows love to live on.

In my journey beyond grief, I've learned that rituals, small intentional acts of remembrance, help bridge the space between what was and what still is. They offer comfort, connection, and a way to honor the love that remains.

Why Rituals Matter in Grief

Grief demands to be felt, and rituals give it a place to exist. They remind us that our loved ones are still part of our lives – not just in the past but in the present. Rituals don't keep us stuck in grief; they help us carry love forward.

I didn't always know how to honor Daquan in a way that felt right. At first, every reminder was painful. But over time, I found small ways to invite his presence into my life — not in a way that kept me tied to the pain, but in a way that let me feel his love more fully.

Creating Your Own Rituals

Rituals don't have to be elaborate. They can be as simple or sacred as you need them to be. Here are some ways I've learned to weave memory into my life:

- **Speaking His Name Aloud** — When I see something that reminds me of him, when I need to feel his presence.

- **Lighting a Candle** — A soft glow in the evening — a reminder that love never fades.

- **Listening to Music That Connects Us** — Certain songs hold his energy, his laughter, his essence. Playing them is a way to bring him close.

- **Spending Time in Nature** — The birds that visit me are more than just birds. They are messengers, reminders that Daquan is never far away.

Your rituals will be your own. The key is finding ways to connect with your loved one in a way that brings peace, not just sorrow.

Holding Space for Memory Without Fear

For a long time, I was afraid of forgetting. I worried that as time passed, his voice in my mind would fade, that his laughter would become distant.

But love, I've learned, does not vanish with time.

Memory is a living thing. The more we engage with it, the more it stays present. We do not have to fear forgetting. Instead, we can choose to remember intentionally.

Love, Forever Woven into Us

Our loved ones may no longer walk beside us, but they are still here, in the way we speak, in the lessons they left us, in the way we carry their love forward.

> *Grief is not about letting go. It's about finding new ways to hold on. It's not an ending, it is a teacher, a mirror, and a love that refuses to vanish.*

Reflection Practice: A Personal Ritual of Remembrance

Take a moment to create your own ritual for honoring your loved one.

1. Choose something meaningful. It can be lighting a candle, saying their name, listening to a song, going for long walks, or writing them a letter. (Whatever feels right for your soul.)

2. Set an intention. Instead of focusing on the loss. Focus on the love.

3. Repeat as needed. Let this be a ritual that brings comfort, not pressure.

Memory is not just looking back; it is keeping love alive in the present. Let your rituals be a bridge between worlds – a way to carry them with you, always.

Reflections:

What emotions, memories, or sensations surfaced?

Take a moment to write whatever arises after practicing your newfound ritual. Let your thoughts unfold onto the page.

No judgement. Just flow.

_____

_____

_____

_____

_____

_____

_____

_____

_____

_____

_____

_____

_____

_____

"

When asked if my cup is half full or half empty, my only response is that I am thankful that I have a cup.

"

- Sam Lefkowitz

Chapter Nine

Gratitude After Grief

G rief and gratitude seem like contradictions. How can you be grateful when your heart is broken? How can you find light when loss has cast a shadow over your world? For a long time, I couldn't. The weight of sorrow was too heavy, the absence too loud. Gratitude felt impossible, maybe even wrong.

But as I moved through my grief, I began to realize that gratitude is not about ignoring pain; it's about recognizing the love that still exists. It's about holding space for both sorrow and appreciation, for both loss and the life that continues to unfold.

Gratitude is Not Erasure

Many people misunderstand gratitude in grief. They think it means "being thankful" that things happened the way they did. But that's not it at all. Gratitude does not erase the pain, and grief does not cancel out gratitude. I've learned to embrace their existence together, side by side.

I am not grateful for my loss. I am grateful for:

The time I had with Daquan, the memories that will never leave me.

The love that remains unbreakable, even beyond this world.

The way grief has opened my heart to deeper connections, to a greater understanding of life's fragility.

The small, everyday moments, the birds that visit, the sun warming my skin, the breath that continues to carry me forward.

Gratitude doesn't mean pretending everything is okay—it means recognizing what remains.

Finding Gratitude in the Little Things

In the depths of grief, gratitude doesn't have to be grand. Sometimes, it's as simple as:

A breath that reminds you you're still here.
A song that brings back a memory.
A friend who checks in, even when you have no words.
A moment of stillness where the weight lifts, if only for a second.

Healing doesn't come all at once. But small moments of gratitude act as steppingstones, leading us forward – little by little

How Gratitude Shifts Grief

Gratitude doesn't take away the pain, but it softens it. It reminds us that even in loss, there is still love. That even in darkness, there is still light.

Grief taught me how fragile life is. But gratitude teaches me how precious it is.

Grief says: "I have lost."

Gratitude says: "I have loved."

Both are true. And in embracing both, we learn to move forward, not by leaving love behind, but by carrying it with us.

Reflection Practice: A Gratitude List for Love That Remains

Take a moment to write down three things you are grateful for today.

They don't have to be big, just something that reminds you that love is still present in your life.

1. Something about your loved one that still lives on (a memory, a lesson, a feeling).

2. Something in nature that reminds you of them.

3. Something within yourself that grief has revealed, a strength, a truth, a deeper love.

Read this list whenever the weight feels unbearable. Grief may change us, but gratitude reminds us that love never truly leaves.

Reflections:

Continue to add to your list with each day. Let gratitude unfold onto the page.

No judgement. Just flow.

_____

_____

_____

_____

_____

_____

_____

_____

_____

_____

_____

_____

_____

_____

_____

_____

_____

Chapter Ten

Beyond Grief – Living & Loving Again

For a long time, I didn't know if life after loss could hold joy again. Grief changes everything; it alters how we see the world, how we love, and how we exist within it. Moving forward felt impossible, as if doing so meant leaving Daquan behind.

But I've come to understand that moving forward does not mean moving away. Healing is not forgetting. Love does not disappear. Instead, it transforms, weaving itself into the fabric of who we are becoming.

Grief may never fully leave us, but neither does love. And at some point, we must decide: Will I allow myself to live again—to love again?

Giving Yourself Permission to Live

One of the hardest parts of grief is allowing yourself to embrace life again without guilt. It's easy to believe that happiness means you've "moved on" or that finding joy is a betrayal of your loss.

Here is my truth: Your loved one would want you to live. They would want you to feel the warmth of the sun, to laugh without hesitation, to love without fear. Your life is still yours to live, and that is not dishonoring them, that is honoring the love they left behind.

Love is Still Available to You

Grief can make us close ourselves off to love, afraid of more loss, more pain. But love is still here, waiting, patient, and asking us to return to it when we're ready.

Loving again, whether through relationships, friendships, or simply embracing life, is not replacing what was lost. It's allowing love to expand, to take new shapes, to remind us that we are still capable of feeling, of giving, and of receiving.

Creating a Future That Honors the Past

Moving beyond grief doesn't mean leaving behind the one you loss. It means integrating their love into the life you are still living.

- *Carry their memory with you in your joys, not just your sorrows.*
- *Let their love inspire the way you show up for yourself and others.*
- *Allow their presence to be felt in the way you continue to grow.*

You are not betraying them by choosing to live. You are carrying them forward with you.

Healing is a Lifelong Journey

There is no destination where grief disappears. But there is a place where it no longer holds you back. Instead, it walks beside you, not as a weight, but as a reminder of the love that shaped you.

"Though grief has changed you. Love remains. And in that love, you can begin again."

Reflection Practice: Opening Yourself to Life Again

Take a deep breath, open your heart, and reflect on these questions:

1. What does living fully look like for me now?

2. How can I honor my loved one while still embracing life?

3. What small step can I take toward joy without guilt?

Write down your answers, knowing that healing is not about leaving love behind – it's about allowing love to lead you forward.

You are still here. You are still allowed to live. And love is still waiting for you.

Let your thoughts unfold onto the page.

No judgement. Just flow.

_____

_____

_____

_____

_____

_____

_____

_____

_____

_____

_____

_____

_____

_____

_____

_____

_____

_____

_____

_____

"Remembering with grace and living with my heart wide open."

Chapter Eleven

Lessons Learned Through Grief

G rief has been my greatest teacher, not because it erased the pain, but because it taught me how to hold it with grace and compassion. Each chapter in this book reflects moments where I felt lost yet, I remembered my way back to myself. These lessons and affirmations are not steps to "complete" healing, but gentle truths that continue to shape how I live, love, and grow.

I share them now, not as instructions, but as gentle reminders that even in sorrow, there is wisdom, strength, and light waiting to unfold. May they hold you, just as they held me.

Love Never Dies

Love doesn't end with loss. It lingers in memories, whispers in the wind, and shows up in unexpected moments – a red bird's visit, a familiar song, or a sudden warmth that reminds me I'm not alone.

Affirm: Love transcends time and space; I carry it always.

Healing is Nonlinear

Grief doesn't move in a straight line. Some days are soft, others sharp, yet every emotion has a place. Healing isn't about erasing pain; it's learning to breathe through it.

Affirm: I honor my pace, trusting that I'm healing even when it feels slow.

Pain Holds Wisdom

I once ran from my pain. But when I stopped resisting and faced it, I found lessons in its depths – resilience, patience, and strength I never knew I had.

Affirm: I allow my pain to teach me, not define me.

Joy is Not Betrayal

For so long, I felt guilty when I laughed or found comfort in the simple beauty of life. But I've learned that joy doesn't dishonor grief – it honors my love by allowing me to live fully.

Affirm: I give myself permission to feel joy without guilt.

Gratitude and Grief Can Coexist

I can miss what's gone and still be thankful for what remains. Grief doesn't cancel gratitude – it deepens it.

Affirm: I hold space for both sorrow and gratitude in my heart.

I Am Still Here, and That Matters

There were days I doubted I would make it through. But each time I chose to get up, breathe, and take one more step forward, I honored my strength.

Affirm: My presence here is enough — I am still standing.

Connection is Healing

Grief can feel isolating, but sharing my story brought me closer to those who understood. Vulnerability opened the door to comfort and connection.

Affirm: I am never alone – love and support surround me always.

Rituals Keep Love Alive

Whether lighting a candle, writing a letter, or speaking Daquan's name, these small acts of remembrance keep his presence close to my heart.

Affirm: I honor my loved one through moments of remembrance.

My Story is Not Over

Grief changed me, but it didn't end me. I am still learning, still growing, still embracing life, one breath, one choice, one moment at a time.

Affirm: I am still becoming — my story continues to unfold.

Strength Grows in Vulnerability

Opening my heart, through tears, truth, and tenderness, has been one of the greatest acts of courage in my healing.

Affirm: My strength is found in allowing myself to feel.

Trust Your Timing

Healing doesn't follow a timeline. I've learned to honor my pace; each slow step is still movement forward.

Affirm: I trust that I am exactly where I need to be.

Nature Heals

The rhythm of the ocean steadied my breath. The sunsets reminded me that endings can be beautiful. Birds became whispers of comfort, reminding me love never leaves.

Affirm: Nature is my sanctuary – its beauty restores me.

Forgiveness Frees the Heart

I carried anger, regret, and guilt until I realized forgiveness wasn't about forgetting, it was about releasing what no longer served me.

Affirm: I release what weighs me down, my heart is free to heal.

Wins Matter

Some days, my greatest victory was simply getting out of bed. I learned to celebrate those quiet moments of courage, each one a quiet act of resilience.

Affirm: Every small step I take is a powerful win.

Embracing Imperfection Brings Peace

Grief is messy. Healing is messy. I've learned that I don't need to get it "right" - I just need to keep going.

Affirm: I embrace my journey with grace and patience.

Your Voice is Powerful

Sharing my story became a lifeline, not just for me, but for others. Speaking my truth turned my pain into purpose.

Affirm: My story has value; my voice brings healing.

The Power of Presence

Grief tried to pull me into the past or future, but I've found my peace by grounding in the present moment.

Affirm: I find comfort by anchoring myself in the here and now.

Hope Can Be Rebuilt

Even when hope felt distant, I found it again in the quiet moments – a sunrise, a smile, a breath. Hope doesn't arrive all at once; sometimes, it flickers back into focus, one spark at a time.

Affirm: I allow hope to find me, no matter how small.

Your Heart Can Hold Both Sorrow and Joy

I once believed my heart couldn't hold both grief and gratitude, but now I know they can coexist. Joy doesn't erase my sadness; it helps me carry it with grace.

Affirm: I make room for both joy and sorrow – my heart is expansive enough for both.

The Journey Continues

Grief does not have an endpoint. There is no final moment where we "get over it" or where loss stops shaping us. But there is a place where it no longer consumes us, where it becomes a part of our story, not the whole story.

For so long, I believed that healing meant saying goodbye. But I now know that grief is not about letting go – it's about learning to hold on differently. It's about carrying love forward, allowing it to expand beyond loss, and giving ourselves permission to keep living.

There are days when the ache still surprises me – softly like a memory brushing past my shoulder, or harder, like a wave pulling me under. I've learned not to fear those moments. They remind me that my grief is valid. That I loved deeply. And that love didn't die – it just changed form.

Grief has taught me how to live with both absence and presence – how to laugh, sometimes with a lump in my throat, how to make space for sorrow without letting it take the whole room. Healing is not a clean line or a perfect arc – it's a spiral. Now when I revisit those places of grief that I thought I moved past. I return with more compassion, more tools, more truth.

The journey isn't about fixing anything. It's about honoring what's real. About rewriting the story with tenderness – not denial. And slowly, piece by piece, life begins to bloom again. Not despite loss, but somehow because of it.

An Invitation to Keep Going

Grief has reshaped me, but it has not erased me. Each lesson has been a reminder that love remains, that healing unfolds in its own time, and that I am stronger than I once believed.

If you are walking this path of grief, know this:

You are not broken.
You are not alone.
And your story, even through the pain, is still unfolding beautifully.

If you are reading this, know that you are still here for a reason. Your story is not over. Your love is not lost. And your healing, however messy, however slow, is unfolding exactly as it needs to.

Take your time. Breathe deeply. Let love lead the way.

Let love be your frequency...

Beyond Grief

Mindful Journaling Prompts

When words feel too heavy to speak, let your pen be your voice. These prompts are here to guide you, to help you release, reflect, and reconnect with yourself. Pause, breathe, and allow each question to open a space within you.

There is no right or wrong way to write ~ only your truth waiting to be discovered. Breathe. Write. Be.

Let your thoughts unfold onto the page.

No judgement, just Flow...

Journal Prompt

Close your eyes, take three slow breaths, and notice your body.

What does grief feel like right now?

No Judgement, just Flow.....

Journal Prompt

Listen to the sounds around you.

Reflect: When you hear the word "loss," what memories or emotions arise?

No Judgement, just Flow.....

Journal Prompt

Inhale deeply, exhale fully.

What has grief taught you about love?

No Judgement, just Flow.....

Journal Prompt

Sit quietly, feeling your tension.

What is the hardest part of sitting with your grief?

No Judgement, just Flow.....

_____

_____

_____

_____

_____

_____

_____

_____

_____

_____

_____

_____

_____

_____

_____

Journal Prompt

Hum a gentle note on your exhale.

If your grief could speak, what would it say?

No Judgement, just Flow.....

_____

_____

_____

_____

_____

_____

_____

_____

_____

_____

_____

_____

_____

_____

_____

_____

Journal Prompt

Visualize your younger self entering grief.

Write a letter to them after a grounding breath.

No Judgement, just Flow.....

Journal Prompt

Take five intentional breaths.

What does "healing" mean to you in this moment?

No Judgement, just Flow.....

Journal Prompt

Place your hand on your chest, breathe, and reflect:

Which memories feel heavy, which feel light?

No Judgement, just Flow.....

Journal Prompt

Close your eyes, listen deeply.

How has grief shifted the way you see the world?

No Judgement, just Flow.....

Journal Prompt

Place your hand over your heart and breathe slowly.

What is one truth about grief you wish others understood?

No Judgement, just Flow.....

_____

_____

_____

_____

_____

_____

_____

_____

_____

_____

_____

_____

_____

_____

_____

_____

Journal Prompt

Inhale for four counts, exhale for six.

How do you define love today, after loss?

No Judgement, just Flow.....

Journal Prompt

Visualize a memory of deep love.

Which memories remind you that love never dies?

No Judgement, just Flow.....

Journal Prompt

Hum softly and feel the vibrations in your chest.

Write about a moment you felt deeply loved.

No Judgement, just Flow.....

Journal Prompt

Place your hand over your heart, breathe fully, and write:

How can you offer yourself unconditional love right now?

No Judgement, just Flow.....

Journal Prompt

Listen to your heartbeat. Reflect:

What role does forgiveness play in your healing journey?

No Judgement, just Flow.....

_____

_____

_____

_____

_____

_____

_____

_____

_____

_____

_____

_____

_____

_____

_____

Journal Prompt

Take three grounding breaths.

In what ways do you resist love—receiving or giving?

No Judgement, just Flow.....

———————————————————————————

———————————————————————————

———————————————————————————

———————————————————————————

———————————————————————————

———————————————————————————

———————————————————————————

———————————————————————————

———————————————————————————

———————————————————————————

———————————————————————————

———————————————————————————

———————————————————————————

———————————————————————————

———————————————————————————

Journal Prompt

Close your eyes and write whatever is on your heart.

No Judgement, just Flow.....

Journal Prompt

Visualize someone or something that brings you comfort.

Write: Who or what helps you feel connected to love when grief feels overwhelming?

No Judgement, just Flow.....

_____

_____

_____

_____

_____

_____

_____

_____

_____

_____

_____

_____

_____

_____

_____

_____

Journal Prompt

Hum or play a gentle sound for 30 seconds.

Recall a moment when grief and love existed together.

No Judgement, just Flow.....

_____

_____

_____

_____

_____

_____

_____

_____

_____

_____

_____

_____

_____

_____

Journal Prompt

Inhale fully, exhale slowly, and write:

How can you honor love daily, even in small ways?

No Judgement, just Flow.....

Journal Prompt

Take five conscious breaths.

Write: What does "healing" look like for you, free from pressure or timelines?

No Judgement, just Flow.....

Journal Prompt

Play a soft sound or hum.

Describe a ritual, practice, or habit that grounds you in difficult moments.

No Judgement, just Flow.....

Journal Prompt

Place your hand on your heart, breathe, and write:

What is one wound you're ready to tend to gently?

No Judgement, just Flow.....

_____

_____

_____

_____

_____

_____

_____

_____

_____

_____

_____

_____

_____

_____

Journal Prompt

Breathe deeply and scan your body.

How do you nurture your body, mind, and spirit?

No Judgement, just Flow.....

Journal Prompt

Close your eyes and notice ambient sounds.

What practices bring you closer to peace?

No Judgement, just Flow.....

Journal Prompt

Take three intentional breaths.

Describe a time when you surprised yourself with your own strength.

No Judgement, just Flow.....

Journal Prompt

Visualize a safe, soft space.

Where in your life could you create more softness?

No Judgement, just Flow.....

Journal Prompt

Breathe slowly and imagine carrying love forward.

How do you honor your loved one in your healing?

No Judgement, just Flow.....

Journal Prompt

Listen deeply to sounds around you.

What sounds, places, or people soothe you when you feel broken open?

No Judgement, just Flow.....

Journal Prompt

Take a few deep breaths.

How does your breath connect you to healing?

No Judgement, just Flow.....

Journal Prompt

Breathe deeply and write:

What new insights about yourself have appeared through grief?

No Judgement, just Flow.....

Journal Prompt

Take a grounding breath.

Which patterns or cycles are you ready to break free from?

No Judgement, just Flow.....

_____

_____

_____

_____

_____

_____

_____

_____

_____

_____

_____

_____

_____

_____

_____

Journal Prompt

Inhale slowly, exhale fully.

How has loss shifted your values or priorities?

No Judgement, just Flow.....

_____

_____

_____

_____

_____

_____

_____

_____

_____

_____

_____

_____

_____

_____

Journal Prompt

Pause, hum....

Describe a moment when growth felt painful but necessary.

No Judgement, just Flow.....

Journal Prompt

Take three intentional breaths.

In what ways are you becoming someone your past self-needed?

No Judgement, just Flow.....

Journal Prompt

Breathe slowly, feel your inner strength.

Which personal strengths have surfaced during your healing journey?

No Judgement, just Flow.....

Journal Prompt

Place your hand on your heart, breathe deeply.

How do you now define resilience?

No Judgement, just Flow.....

Journal Prompt

Inhale fully, exhale slowly.

What are you learning about surrender?

No Judgement, just Flow.....

Journal Prompt

Listen to gentle ambient sounds.

Describe a moment where growth and gratitude coexisted.

No Judgement, just Flow.....

_____

_____

_____

_____

_____

_____

_____

_____

_____

_____

_____

_____

_____

_____

Journal Prompt

Take five grounding breaths.

What does "beyond grief" look like to you?

No Judgement, just Flow.....

_____

_____

_____

_____

_____

_____

_____

_____

_____

_____

_____

_____

_____

_____

_____

Journal Prompt

Close your eyes and breathe deeply.

What practices help you reconnect with joy?

No Judgement, just Flow.....

Journal Prompt

Visualize your favorite natural place.

Describe a place in nature that feels healing to you.

No Judgement, just Flow.....

Journal Prompt

Take a slow breath in, exhale fully.

What new dreams or possibilities are opening within you?

No Judgement, just Flow.....

_____

_____

_____

_____

_____

_____

_____

_____

_____

_____

_____

_____

_____

_____

_____

_____

Journal Prompt

Listen to your heartbeat for a moment.

How can you invite more gratitude into your daily life?

No Judgement, just Flow.....

_____

_____

_____

_____

_____

_____

_____

_____

_____

_____

_____

_____

_____

_____

_____

_____

Journal Prompt

Breathe fully and exhale slowly.

What does peace mean to you today?

No Judgement, just Flow.....

Journal Prompt

Visualize a symbol that represents your journey.

Which symbol best reflects your healing process?

No Judgement, just Flow.....

Journal Prompt

Take three grounding breaths.

How do you want to carry your loved one's memory forward?

No Judgement, just Flow.....

Journal Prompt

Hum or play a gentle sound.

What does a life lived in alignment with love look like for you?

No Judgement, just Flow.....

_____

_____

_____

_____

_____

_____

_____

_____

_____

_____

_____

_____

_____

_____

_____

_____

Journal Prompt

Inhale fully, exhale slowly.

What kind of future are you building through your healing?

No Judgement, just Flow.....

Journal Prompt

Close your eyes, place your hand on your heart, and breathe.

Create your own affirmation or mantra you can return to when grief resurfaces.

No Judgement, just Flow.....

About the Author

Mina Moore, born Taromina, is a free spirit, soul-healer, and storyteller whose journey through grief became the soil for her deepest growth. Rooted in the rhythms of nature, she finds joy in gardening, sunrise meditations, barefoot walks, and stargazing under wide open skies.

Her path has been one of both heartbreak and awakening. After the passing of her son, Daquan, she was cracked open—and from that place, she began to pick up the pieces and rebuild her life through love, compassion, and presence.

For most of her life, she was known as Taromina—a name wrapped in the expectations of others. But after the heartbreaking loss of her beloved son, she began to write under the name Mina Moore, a sacred reclamation of self. Mina represents the woman she is becoming, healing, whole, and no longer confined to people-pleasing or performing.

A writer since childhood, Mina has always found refuge in words—crafting short stories and poetry to express what couldn't be spoken aloud. Writing became her sanctuary, her compass, and her healing.

As an author, sound healing facilitator, Reiki practitioner, and grief companion, Mina blends energy work with storytelling and soul-centered practices to hold space for others to feel, breathe, and evolve. Her work is rooted in raw honesty, tender reflection, and the belief that healing is a lifelong journey of remembering who we truly are.

Her work is inspired by nature, the wisdom found in quiet moments, and the strength born from personal transformation. Mina cares deeply about guiding others on the journey through and Beyond Grief—back home to themselves, where power, presence, and peace reside.

Community

This journey is not meant to be walked alone. When you join my community, you'll receive gentle reminders of love and support through my newsletter—reflections, meditations, and invitations to workshops and sound journeys. Together, we move forward in healing, always returning to love.

Follow me here:
Instagram: minamooresoundfeels

Your path to transformation begins within

Ready to begin your journey? Scan the QR code to visit minamoore.com to explore Sound healing resources for grief, guided meditations, and other supportive practices to deepen your self-healing journey.

Together we rise in Vibration
One Sound One Breath at a Time.
The frequency is LOVE...

Made in the USA
Middletown, DE
20 November 2025

22461743R00086